GREAT MINDS® WIT & WISDOM

Grade 1 Module 3:
Powerful Forces

Student Edition

COPYRIGHT STATEMENT

Published by Great Minds®.

Copyright ©2016 Great Minds®. All rights reserved. No part of this work may be reproduced or used in any form or by any means—graphic, electronic, or mechanical, including photocopying or information storage and retrieval systems—without written permission from the copyright holder.

ISBN: 978-1-68386-023-5

Table of Contents

Handout 1A: Fluency Homework

Handout 1B: Shades of Meaning Chart

Handout 3A: Buttons and Boxes

Handout 3B: Wind Illustration

Handout 5A: Research Evidence Organizer

Handout 7A: Topic Sandwich Chart

Handout 7B: Informative Writing Checklist

Handout 8A: Fluency Homework

Handout 10A: Write a Problem

Handout 11A: *Feelings* Story Map

Handout 12A: Narrative Writing Checklist

Handout 12B: Shades of Meaning Chart

Handout 13A: Fluency Homework

Handout 15A: Gilberto and the Balloon

Handout 16A: Word Cards

Handout 17A: Fluency Homework

Handout 17B: Verb-Tense Chart

Handout 18A: "The Guest" Story Map

Handout 18B: Focusing Question Task 3 Story Map

Handout 18C: Root Words

Handout 19A: Narrative Writing Checklist

Handout 21A: Fluency Homework

Handout 22A: *Brave Irene* Story Map

Handout 23A: *Brave Irene* Scene

Handout 23B: Word Cards

Handout 24A: *Brave Irene* Evidence Organizer

Handout 26A: Fluency Homework

Handout 27A: Key Events

Handout 27B: A Scene about William

Handout 28A: *The Boy Who Harnessed the Wind* Evidence Organizer

Handout 28B: Prefixes

Handout 32A: End-of-Module Story Map

Handout 33A: Story Element Icons

Handout 34A: Narrative Writing Checklist

Handout 35A: Socratic Seminar Self-Assessment

Volume of Reading Reflection Questions

Wit & Wisdom Parent Tip Sheet

Name:

Handout 1A: Fluency Homework

Directions: Read the text for homework. Have an adult or peer initial the unshaded boxes each day that you read the passage.

Feel the Wind, Arthur Dorros

Wind is moving air. Air is what we breathe. It is everywhere around us, even though we can't see it. We can't see air. And we can't really see wind. But we can see the wind move things. Wind pushes clouds across the sky. Wind flutters leaves of trees and makes ripples on the lake.

55 Words

Dorros, Arthur. *Feel the Wind*. HarperCollins, 1989.

Student Performance Checklist:	Day 1		Day 2		Day 3	
	You	Listener*	You	Listener*	You	Listener*
Read the passage three to five times.						
Read with appropriate phrasing and pausing.						
Read with appropriate expression.						
Read at a good pace, not too fast and not too slow.						
Read to be heard and understood.						

*Adult or peer

Name:

Feel the Wind, Arthur Dorros

Wind is moving air. Air is what we breathe. It is everywhere around us, even though we can't see it. We can't see air. And we can't really see wind. But we can see the wind move things. Wind pushes clouds across the sky. Wind flutters leaves of trees and makes ripples on the lake.

55 Words

Dorros, Arthur. *Feel the Wind*. HarperCollins, 1989.

Student Performance Checklist:	Day 4		Day 5		Day 6	
	You	Listener*	You	Listener*	You	Listener*
Read the passage three to five times.						
Read with appropriate phrasing and pausing.						
Read with appropriate expression.						
Read at a good pace, not too fast and not too slow.						
Read to be heard and understood.						

*Adult or peer

Name:

Handout 1B: Shades of Meaning Chart

Directions: Place the verbs from the poem on the chart from least strong to strongest.

Name: _____

Handout 3A: Buttons and Boxes

Directions: Cut on dotted lines. Say a detail and place a button in the box.

Name:

Handout 3B: Wind Illustration

Directions: Study the illustration to answer the question, "What can I learn about wind from studying this illustration?"

Name:

Handout 5A: Research Evidence Organizer

Directions: Record key details about what the wind can do during a hurricane to complete the Evidence Organizer.

	Source 1: *Feel the Wind*	Source 3:
Key Details		

Name:

Handout 7A: Topic Sandwich Chart

Directions: Point to each component of the Topic Sandwich as you orally rehearse an informative paragraph.

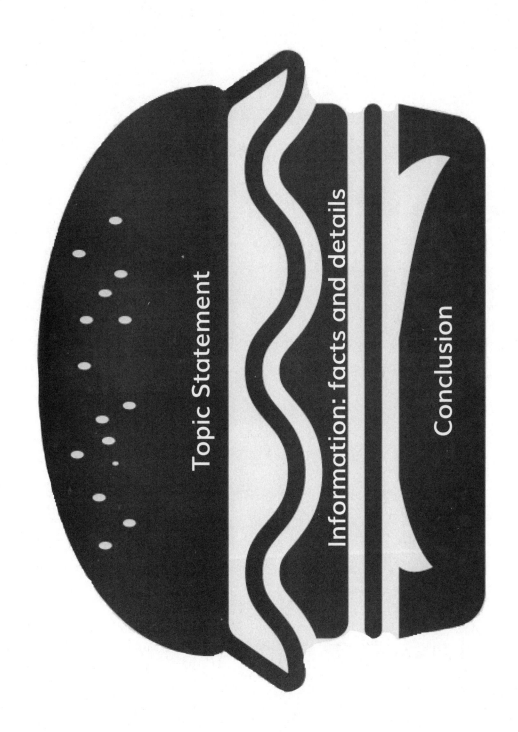

Name:

Handout 7B: Informative Writing Checklist

Directions: Circle ☺ Yes or ☹ Not Yet to answer each prompt.

Grade 1 Informative Writing Checklist			
Structure	**Self**	**Peer**	**Teacher**
I have a topic statement that names my topic.	☺ ☹ Yes Not Yet	☺ ☹ Yes Not Yet	☺ ☹ Yes Not Yet
I have two or more facts or details to support my topic statement.	☺ ☹ Yes Not Yet	☺ ☹ Yes Not Yet	☺ ☹ Yes Not Yet
I have a conclusion.	☺ ☹ Yes Not Yet	☺ ☹ Yes Not Yet	☺ ☹ Yes Not Yet
Conventions	**Self**	**Peer**	**Teacher**
I use capital letters at the beginning of sentences and proper nouns. **ABC**	☺ ☹ Yes Not Yet	☺ ☹ Yes Not Yet	☺ ☹ Yes Not Yet

Name:

I use end punctuation. . ? !	☺ ☹ Yes Not Yet	☺ ☹ Yes Not Yet	☺ ☹ Yes Not Yet
I write complete sentences.	☺ ☹ Yes Not Yet	☺ ☹ Yes Not Yet	☺ ☹ Yes Not Yet
I use my best spelling.	☺ ☹ Yes Not Yet	☺ ☹ Yes Not Yet	☺ ☹ Yes Not Yet
Total number of ☺			

Name:

Handout 8A: Fluency Homework

Directions: Choose one of the text options to read for homework. Have an adult or peer initial the unshaded boxes each day that you read the passage.

Option A

"Whiskers," Aliki

Girl: Whiskers died.
Boy: Oh, poor Whiskers. You had her so long. I'm sad for you.

Girl: She was old. She was sick.
She had to die sometime. My heart is broken.

Boy: She was silly.
Girl: She was funny.
Both: We'll miss you, Whiskers.

46 Words

Aliki. *Feelings*. HarperCollins, 1984.

Student Performance Checklist:	Day 1		Day 2		Day 3		Day 4	
	You	Listener*	You	Listener*	You	Listener*	You	Listener*
Read the passage three to five times.								
Read with appropriate phrasing and pausing.								

Name:

Student Performance Checklist:	Day 1		Day 2		Day 3		Day 4	
	You	Listener*	You	Listener*	You	Listener*	You	Listener*
Read with appropriate expression.								
Read at a good pace, not too fast and not too slow.								
Read to be heard and understood.								

*Adult or peer

Name:

Option B

"Your Attention, Please," Aliki

Mom: Look at Adam run.
Girl: I can run faster.

Mom: Look at Adam build.
Girl: I can build higher.

Mom: Listen to Adam.
Girl: Listen to me.

Mom: Adam can read.
Girl: I can read more.

Mom: Ha Ha Ha Ha. Adam is funny!
Girl: Ha Ha Ha Ha. I am funny, too.

Mom: Where is Adam?!
Girl: Where am I?

Mom: Adam is hurt!
Girl: I'm hurt, too.

Mom: Look at Adam!
Girl: Look at me!

Mom: I see you, dear. You're wonderful.

85 Words

Aliki. *Feelings*. HarperCollins, 1984.

Name:

Student Performance Checklist:	Day 1		Day 2		Day 3		Day 4	
	You	Listener*	You	Listener*	You	Listener*	You	Listener*
Read the passage three to five times.								
Read with appropriate phrasing and pausing.								
Read with appropriate expression.								
Read at a good pace, not too fast and not too slow.								
Read to be heard and understood.								

*Adult or peer

Handout 10A: Write a Problem

Directions: Complete each Sentence Frame. Write a character's name, setting, and a problem to complete the partial story.

One night _____.

_____ was in his _____.

Suddenly, _____
_____.

Name:

started to

cry.

Name:

Handout 11A: *Feelings* Story Map

Directions: Draw a picture or write to show the elements of the story.

Feelings

Characters	Setting
Problem	
Resolution	

Name:

Handout 12A: Narrative Writing Checklist

Directions: Circle 😊 Yes or 😐 Not Yet to answer each prompt.

Grade 1 Narrative Writing Checklist			
Structure	Self	Peer	Teacher
I have characters.	😊 Yes 😐 Not Yet	😊 Yes 😐 Not Yet	😊 Yes 😐 Not Yet
I have a setting.	😊 Yes 😐 Not Yet	😊 Yes 😐 Not Yet	😊 Yes 😐 Not Yet
I have a problem.	😊 Yes 😐 Not Yet	😊 Yes 😐 Not Yet	😊 Yes 😐 Not Yet
I have time-order words to sequence two or more events. (One day, Suddenly, Then)	😊 Yes 😐 Not Yet	😊 Yes 😐 Not Yet	😊 Yes 😐 Not Yet
I have a resolution.	😊 Yes 😐 Not Yet	😊 Yes 😐 Not Yet	😊 Yes 😐 Not Yet

Name:

Conventions	Self	Peer	Teacher
I use capital letters at the beginning of sentences and proper nouns. **ABC**	☺ ☹ Yes Not Yet	☺ ☹ Yes Not Yet	☺ ☹ Yes Not Yet
I use end punctuation. **. ? !**	☺ ☹ Yes Not Yet	☺ ☹ Yes Not Yet	☺ ☹ Yes Not Yet
I use complete sentences.	☺ ☹ Yes Not Yet	☺ ☹ Yes Not Yet	☺ ☹ Yes Not Yet
I use words to describe the character's feelings.	☺ ☹ Yes Not Yet	☺ ☹ Yes Not Yet	☺ ☹ Yes Not Yet

Name: _____

Handout 12B: Shades of Meaning Chart

Directions: Write the words from the class chart from sad to heartbroken.

sad
heartbroken

Name:

Handout 13A: Fluency Homework

Directions: Read the text for homework. Have an adult or peer initial the unshaded boxes each day that you read the passage.

Gilberto and the Wind, Marie Hall Ets

I hear Wind whispering at the door. "You-ou-ou," he whispers. "You-ou-ou-ou!" So I get my balloon, and I run out to play.

At first Wind is gentle and just floats my balloon around in the air. But then, with a jerk, he grabs it away and carries it up to the top of a tree. "Wind! Oh, Wind!" I say. "Blow it back to me! Please!" But he won't. He just laughs and whispers, "You-ou-ou-ou!"

75 Words

Ets, Marie Hall. *Gilberto and the Wind*. Viking, 1963.

Student Performance Checklist:	Day 1		Day 2		Day 3		Day 4	
	You	Listener*	You	Listener*	You	Listener*	You	Listener*
Read the passage three to five times.								
Read with appropriate phrasing and pausing.								
Read with appropriate expression.								
Read at a good pace, not too fast and not too slow.								
Read to be heard and understood.								

*Adult or peer

Name: _____

Handout 15A: Gilberto and the Balloon

Directions: Cut on the dotted lines. Glue the story to a sheet of paper. Listen carefully as your teacher reads the story. Select two ways Gilberto responds to the problem. Glue your responses below the story.

Gilberto is in the yard playing with his balloon. Suddenly, Wind grabs the balloon and carries it to the top of the tree. Gilberto is angry.

Gilberto walks to the tree and jumps to grab the string.

Gilberto pops the balloon.

Gilberto bangs the branch with a stick.

Name:

Handout 16A: Word Cards

Directions: Cut apart the word cards.

gentle	strong
shakes	carries
floats	jerks
grabs	pull
breaks	

Name:

Handout 17A: Fluency Homework

Directions: Read the text for homework. Have an adult or peer initial the unshaded boxes each day that you read the passage.

"The Guest," Arnold Lobel

Page 5
Narrator: Owl was at home.

Owl: How good it feels to be sitting by this fire. It is so cold and snowy outside.

Narrator: Owl was eating buttered toast and hot pea soup for supper.

Narrator: Owl heard a loud sound at the front door.

Owl: Who is out there, banging and pounding at my door on a night like this?

Narrator: Owl opened the door. No one was there. Only the snow and wind.

Page 13
Narrator: The snow whirled up the stairs and whooshed down the hallway.

Owl: Winter! You are my guest. This is no way to behave!

Name:

Narrator: But Winter did not listen. It made the window shades flap and shiver. It turned the pea soup into hard, green ice.

Narrator: Winter went into all the rooms of Owl's house. Soon everything was covered with snow.

Owl: You must go, Winter! Go away, right now!

67 Words

Lobel, Arnold. "The Guest." *Owl at Home*, HarperCollins, 1975.

Student Performance Checklist:	Day 1		Day 2		Day 3		Day 4	
	You	Listener*	You	Listener*	You	Listener*	You	Listener*
Read the passage three to five times.								
Read with appropriate phrasing and pausing.								
Read with appropriate expression.								
Read at a good pace, not too fast and not too slow.								
Read to be heard and understood.								

*Adult or peer

Name: _____

Handout 17B: Verb-Tense Chart

Directions: Fill in the chart.

Verb Tenses		
Past	**Present**	**Future**
-ed	-ing	will _____

Name: _____

Handout 18A: "The Guest" Story Map

Directions: Draw a picture or write to show the elements of the story.

"The Guest"

Characters	Setting

Problem

Responses to the Problem

Name:

Resolution

Name: _____

Handout 18B: Focusing Question Task 3 Story Map

Directions: Draw a picture or write to show the elements of the story.

"The Guest"

Characters	Setting
Owl	Owl's House

Problem

Name:

Responses to the Problem

Resolution

Name: _____

Handout 18C: Root Words

Directions: Find the ending and cut apart each card to find the root word.

thumped	bumped
behaved	jerked
shivered	pushed

Name:

Handout 19A: Narrative Writing Checklist

Directions: Circle ☺ Yes or ☹ Not Yet to answer each prompt.

Grade 1 Narrative Writing Checklist			
Structure	Self	Peer	Teacher
I have characters.	☺ ☹ Yes Not Yet	☺ ☹ Yes Not Yet	☺ ☹ Yes Not Yet
I have a setting.	☺ ☹ Yes Not Yet	☺ ☹ Yes Not Yet	☺ ☹ Yes Not Yet
I have a problem.	☺ ☹ Yes Not Yet	☺ ☹ Yes Not Yet	☺ ☹ Yes Not Yet
I have time-order words to sequence two or more events. (One day, Suddenly, Then)	☺ ☹ Yes Not Yet	☺ ☹ Yes Not Yet	☺ ☹ Yes Not Yet

Name:

	Self	Peer	Teacher
I have two or more ways a character responds to the problem.	☺ ☹ Yes Not Yet	☺ ☹ Yes Not Yet	☺ ☹ Yes Not Yet
I have a resolution.	☺ ☹ Yes Not Yet	☺ ☹ Yes Not Yet	☺ ☹ Yes Not Yet
Conventions	**Self**	**Peer**	**Teacher**
I use capital letters at the beginning of sentences and proper nouns. **ABC**	☺ ☹ Yes Not Yet	☺ ☹ Yes Not Yet	☺ ☹ Yes Not Yet
I use end punctuation. . ? !	☺ ☹ Yes Not Yet	☺ ☹ Yes Not Yet	☺ ☹ Yes Not Yet
I use complete sentences.	☺ ☹ Yes Not Yet	☺ ☹ Yes Not Yet	☺ ☹ Yes Not Yet
I use words to describe the character's feelings.	☺ ☹ Yes Not Yet	☺ ☹ Yes Not Yet	☺ ☹ Yes Not Yet
I use present-tense verbs.	☺ ☹ Yes Not Yet	☺ ☹ Yes Not Yet	☺ ☹ Yes Not Yet

Name:

Handout 21A: Fluency Homework

Directions: Read the text for homework. Have an adult or peer initial the unshaded boxes each day that you read the passage.

"It Fell in the City," Eve Merriam

It fell in the city,
It fell through the night,
And the black rooftops
All turned white.

Red fire hydrants
All turned white.
Blue police cars
All turned white.

Green garbage cans
All turned white.
Gray sidewalks
All turned white.

Yellow NO PARKING signs
All turned white
When it fell in the city
All through the night.

57 Words

Handout 21A: "It Fell in the City" From BLACKBERRY INK by Eve Merriam. Copyright © 1985 Eve Merriam. All Rights Renewed and Reserved. Used by permission of Marian Reiner.

Name:

Student Performance Checklist:	Day 1		Day 2		Day 3		Day 4		Day 5	
	You	Listener*	You	Listener*	You	Listener*	You	Listener*	You	Listener*
Read the passage three to five times.										
Read with appropriate phrasing and pausing.	▓	▓								
Read with appropriate expression.	▓	▓	▓	▓						
Read at a good pace, not too fast and not too slow.	▓	▓	▓	▓	▓	▓				
Read to be heard and understood.	▓	▓	▓	▓	▓	▓				

*Adult or peer

Name: _____

Handout 22A: *Brave Irene* Story Map

Directions: Draw a picture or write to show the elements of the story.

Brave Irene

Characters	Setting

Problem

Responses to the Problem

Name:

Resolution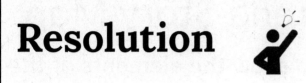

Name: _____

Handout 23A: *Brave Irene* Scene

Directions: Use sensory and feelings words to complete each sentence in the scene.

The _____ wind pushed Irene to the ground.

She was _____ and _____.

Irene stood up. She felt _____.

Irene yelled, "Get out of my way!"

Name:

Handout 23B: Word Cards

Directions: Cut apart the word cards.

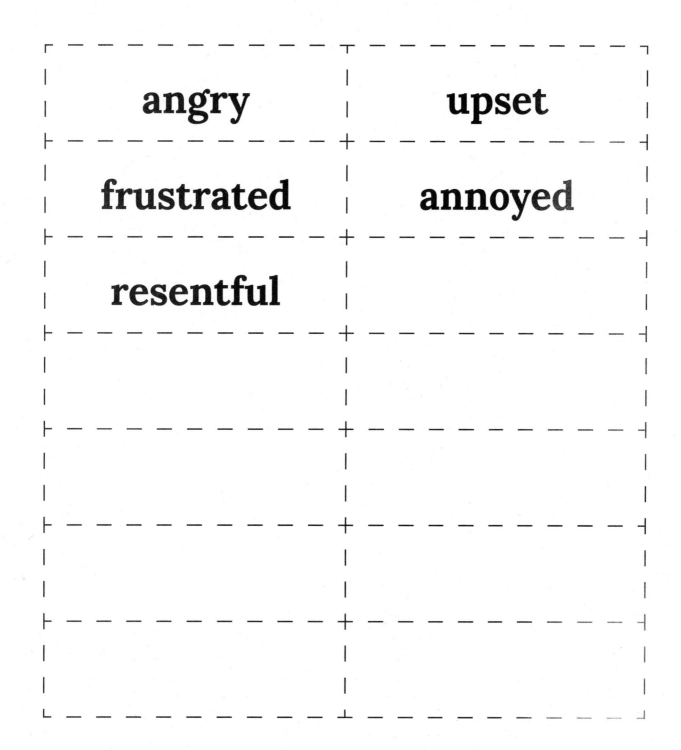

Name: _____

Handout 24A: *Brave Irene* Evidence Organizer

Directions: Circle a scene from *Brave Irene* to write about.

Choice 1: "the wind drove Irene along so rudely …"
Choice 2: "the ill-tempered wind ripped the box open …"

Write sensory and feelings words to describe:

- What Irene saw, heard, and felt during the scene.

- How Irene felt, in terms of her emotions, during the scene.

Saw	Heard	Felt or Touched

A word to describe how Irene felt during this scene

Name:

Handout 26A: Fluency Homework

Directions: Read the text for homework. Have an adult or peer initial the unshaded boxes each day that you read the passage.

> "The Wind," James Reeves
>
> I can get through a doorway without any key,
> And strip the leaves from the great oak tree,
> I can drive storm-clouds and shake tall towers,
> Or steal through a garden and not wake the flowers.
> Seas I can move and ships I can sink;
> I can carry a house-top or the scent of a pink.
> When I am angry I can rave and riot;
> and when I am spent, I lie quiet as quiet.
>
> 75 Words
>
> Reeves, James. "The Wind." *Lower School Poetry Archive*, Web. Accessed 15 Sept. 2016.

Name:

Student Performance Checklist:	Day 1		Day 2		Day 3	
	You	Listener*	You	Listener*	You	Listener*
Read the passage three to five times.						
Read with appropriate phrasing and pausing.						
Read with appropriate expression.						
Read at a good pace, not too fast and not too slow.						
Read to be heard and understood.						

Student Performance Checklist:	Day 4		Day 5		Day 6	
	You	Listener*	You	Listener*	You	Listener*
Read the passage three to five times.						
Read with appropriate phrasing and pausing.						
Read with appropriate expression.						
Read at a good pace, not too fast and not too slow.						
Read to be heard and understood.						

*Adult or peer

Name:

Handout 27A: Key Events

Directions: Cut apart the key events cards. Sequence the events and retell the story.

Name:

Name: _____

Handout 27B: A Scene about William

Directions: Fill in the blanks with sensory and feelings words to complete the scene on page 15 from *The Boy Who Harnessed the Wind*.

In the junkyard, pieces appeared like

_____ treasures

in the _____ grass.

William felt_____.

Name:

Handout 28A: *The Boy Who Harnessed the Wind* Evidence Organizer

Directions: Write sensory and feelings words to describe the scene on pages 21–22 from *The Boy Who Harnessed the Wind*:

- What William saw, heard, and felt during the scene.

- How William felt, in terms of his emotions, during the scene.

Saw 	Heard	Felt or Touched

A word to describe how William felt during this scene

Name: _____

Handout 28B: Prefixes

Directions: Write the prefix in front of the word to create a new word that matches the definition.

____mix mix before	____tie tie again
____made made again	____cook cook before
____pay pay before	____pack pack again
____write write again	____mix mix again

Name: _____

Handout 32A: End-of-Module Story Map

Directions: Draw a picture or write to show the elements of the story.

Characters	Setting

Problem

Responses to the Problem

Name: _____

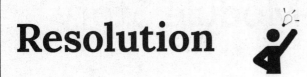

Name:

Handout 33A: Story Element Icons

Directions: Cut out and glue these icons to End-of-Module writing paper to help plan your story.

Name:

Handout 34A: Narrative Writing Checklist

Directions: Circle ☺ Yes or ☹ Not Yet to answer each prompt.

Grade 1 Narrative Writing Checklist			
Structure	Self	Peer	Teacher
I have characters.	☺ ☹ Yes Not Yet	☺ ☹ Yes Not Yet	☺ ☹ Yes Not Yet
I have a setting.	☺ ☹ Yes Not Yet	☺ ☹ Yes Not Yet	☺ ☹ Yes Not Yet
I have a problem.	☺ ☹ Yes Not Yet	☺ ☹ Yes Not Yet	☺ ☹ Yes Not Yet
I have time-order words to sequence two or more events. (One day, Suddenly, Then)	☺ ☹ Yes Not Yet	☺ ☹ Yes Not Yet	☺ ☹ Yes Not Yet

Name:

	Self	Peer	Teacher
I have two or more ways a character responds to the problem.	☺ ☹ Yes Not Yet	☺ ☹ Yes Not Yet	☺ ☹ Yes Not Yet
I have a resolution.	☺ ☹ Yes Not Yet	☺ ☹ Yes Not Yet	☺ ☹ Yes Not Yet
Conventions	**Self**	**Peer**	**Teacher**
I use capital letters at the beginning of sentences and proper nouns. **ABC**	☺ ☹ Yes Not Yet	☺ ☹ Yes Not Yet	☺ ☹ Yes Not Yet
I use end punctuation. **. ? !**	☺ ☹ Yes Not Yet	☺ ☹ Yes Not Yet	☺ ☹ Yes Not Yet
I use complete sentences.	☺ ☹ Yes Not Yet	☺ ☹ Yes Not Yet	☺ ☹ Yes Not Yet
I use words to describe the character's feelings.	☺ ☹ Yes Not Yet	☺ ☹ Yes Not Yet	☺ ☹ Yes Not Yet
I use sensory words.	☺ ☹ Yes Not Yet	☺ ☹ Yes Not Yet	☺ ☹ Yes Not Yet

Name: _____

Handout 35A: Socratic Seminar Self-Assessment

Directions: Use one of the letters below to describe how often you performed each action during the Socratic Seminar.

A = I always did that.
S = I sometimes did that.
N = I'll do that next time.

Expectation	Evaluation (A, S, N)
I followed our class rules for the seminar.	
I asked and answered questions to gather or clarify information.	
I spoke in complete sentences.	
I readied my body to listen.	
I listened with my whole body.	

Volume of Reading Reflection Questions

Powerful Forces, Grade 1, Module 3

Student Name:

Text:

Author:

Topic:

Genre/type of book:

Share what you know about the wind by sharing the answers to the questions. Draw, write, or tell your teacher your answers.

Informational Texts

1. **Wonder:** What do you notice when you look at the title and illustrations on the cover of this book? How is this book different from a story?

2. **Organize:** What does the author tell you about wind in this book? What are the main ideas of the text?

3. **Reveal:** How does the illustrator or photographer show you more about the wind? Find one place in the text where you learn an important detail from an illustration. What is the detail that you learned?

4. **Distill:** What is the most important idea about wind that you learned by reading this text? Draw a picture showing this idea and explain your drawing on the paper or to your teacher.

5. **Know:** What new information do you now know about the wind? Explain how this information compares to a different book about wind. Is it the same or is it different information? Explain.

6. **Vocabulary:** What new word from this book would you like to learn to use? What clues in the text or illustrations might help you know what it means? Ask an adult to help you figure out the meaning. Create a drawing and a sentence that shows the new word and its meaning.

Literary Texts

1. **Wonder:** Look at the title and illustrations on the cover. What do you wonder about the story? How is this book different from an informational text?

2. **Organize:** What happened in this story? Act out the story focusing on how the character feels. Be sure your face looks like the character feels during the beginning, middle, and end of the story.

3. **Reveal:** How does the author use sensory details to tell us more of the story? Find one sensory detail and explain how you learned more about a story part because of the detail.

4. **Distill:** Did any of the characters in this story learn a lesson? What lesson did they learn?

5. **Know:** How do the characters in this story tell you more about people's feelings? What made their feelings change?

6. **Vocabulary:** What are three words or phrases that suggest feelings? Make up motions to go with each feeling or draw faces to show the expression that goes with the feeling. Be sure to write the words or phrases with your picture.

WIT & WISDOM PARENT TIP SHEET

WHAT IS MY GRADE 1 STUDENT LEARNING IN MODULE 3?

Wit & Wisdom is our English curriculum. It builds knowledge of key topics in history, science, and literature through the study of excellent texts. By reading and responding to stories and nonfiction texts, we will build knowledge of the following topics:

Module 1: A World of Books

Module 2: Creature Features

Module 3: Powerful Forces

Module 4: Cinderella Stories

In Module 3, *Powerful Forces*, students discover the capacity of wind and the emotions it evokes. We will ask: How do people respond to the powerful force of the wind?

OUR CLASS WILL READ THESE BOOKS:

Picture Books (Literary)

- *Brave Irene*, William Steig
- *Owl at Home*, Arnold Lobel, "The Guest"
- *Gilberto and the Wind*, Marie Hall Ets

Picture Books (Informational)

- *The Boy Who Harnessed the Wind*, William Kamkwamba and Bryan Mealer
- *Feel the Wind*, Arthur Dorros
- *Feelings*, Aliki

Poetry

- "The Wind," James Reeves
- "It Fell in the City," Eve Merriam
- "This Windmill," Amy Ludwig VanDerwater

OUR CLASS WILL WATCH THESE VIDEOS:

- "William and the Windmill," *Toronto Star*

OUR CLASS WILL READ THESE ARTICLES:

- "Wind at Work"
- "What Makes the Wind?"

OUR CLASS WILL READ THIS SHORT STORY EXCERPT:

- "Owl and the Moon," Arnold Lobel

OUR CLASS WILL EXAMINE THESE PAINTINGS:

- *The Red Mill*, Piet Mondrian (1911)
- *Oostzijdse Mill with Extended Blue, Yellow and Purple Sky*, Piet Mondrian (1907)
- *Windmill in the Gein*, Piet Mondrian (1906–7)

OUR CLASS WILL ASK THESE QUESTIONS:

- How is wind a powerful force?
- What are feelings?
- How do characters respond to the powerful force of the wind?
- How does Irene respond to the powerful force of the wind?
- How does William use the powerful force of the wind?

QUESTIONS TO ASK AT HOME:

As you read with your Grade 1 student, ask:

- What is the essential meaning, or most important message, in this book?

BOOKS TO READ AT HOME:

- *The Wonderful Wizard of Oz*, L. Frank Baum
- *Alexander and the Terrible, Horrible, No Good, Very Bad Day*, Judith Viorst
- *Coppernickel Goes Mondrian*, Wouter van Reek
- *Time of Wonder*, Robert McCloskey
- *Katy and the Big Snow*, Virginia Lee Burton
- *A Small Tall Tale from the Far Far North*, Peter Sís

- *Hurricanes!*, Gail Gibbons
- *Tornadoes!*, Gail Gibbons
- *The Wind Blew*, Pat Hutchins

PLACES YOU CAN VISIT TO TALK ABOUT THE WIND:
- Visit a nearby park or go for a walk together on a windy day.
- Sit near an open window to feel the breeze.
- Take a trip to the beach if you live nearby.

ASK:
- What do you know about the wind?
- What does the wind feel like?
- What does the wind sound like?
- Can you see the wind?
- How does this weather make you feel?
- What activities do you like to do on a windy day?
- What can the wind help you do?

CREDITS

Great Minds® has made every effort to obtain permission for the reprinting of all copyrighted material. If any owner of copyrighted material is not acknowledged herein, please contact Great Minds® for proper acknowledgment in all future editions and reprints of this module.

- All images are used under license from Shutterstock.com unless otherwise noted.

- All material from the *Common Core State Standards for English Language Arts & Literacy in History/Social Studies, Science, and Technical Subjects* © Copyright 2010 National Governors Association Center for Best Practices and Council of Chief State School Officers. All rights reserved.

- Handout 21A: "It Fell in the City" From BLACKBERRY INK by Eve Merriam. Copyright © 1985 Eve Merriam. All Rights Renewed and Reserved. Used by permission of Marian Reiner.

- Assessment 17A: "Wind at Work" from *When the Wind Blows*, Click magazine, March 2012. Text copyright © 2012 by Carus Publishing Company. Reprinted by permission of Cricket Media. All Cricket Media material is copyrighted by Carus Publishing d/b/a Cricket Media, and/or various authors and illustrators. Any commercial use or distribution of material without permission is strictly prohibited. Please visit **http://www.cricketmedia.com/info/licensing2** for licensing and **http://www.cricketmedia.com** for subscriptions

- Assessment 31A: "What Makes the Wind?" from *When the Wind Blows*, Click magazine, March 2012. Text copyright © 2012 by Carus Publishing Company. Reprinted by permission of Cricket Media. All Cricket Media material is copyrighted by Carus Publishing d/b/a Cricket Media, and/or various authors and illustrators. Any commercial use or distribution of material without permission is strictly prohibited. Please visit **http://www.cricketmedia.com/info/licensing2** for licensing and **http://www.cricketmedia.com** for subscriptions

- For updated credit information, please visit **http://witeng.link/credits**.

ACKNOWLEDGMENTS

Great Minds® Staff

The following writers, editors, reviewers, and support staff contributed to the development of this curriculum.

Ann Brigham, Lauren Chapalee, Sara Clarke, Emily Climer, Lorraine Griffith, Emily Gula, Sarah Henchey, Trish Huerster, Stephanie Kane-Mainier, Lior Klirs, Liz Manolis, Andrea Minich, Lynne Munson, Marya Myers, Rachel Rooney, Aaron Schifrin, Danielle Shylit, Rachel Stack, Sarah Turnage, Michelle Warner, Amy Wierzbicki, Margaret Wilson, and Sarah Woodard.

Colleagues and Contributors

We are grateful for the many educators, writers, and subject-matter experts who made this program possible.

David Abel, Robin Agurkis, Elizabeth Bailey, Julianne Barto, Amy Benjamin, Andrew Biemiller, Charlotte Boucher, Sheila Byrd-Carmichael, Eric Carey, Jessica Carloni, Janine Cody, Rebecca Cohen, Elaine Collins, Tequila Cornelious, Beverly Davis, Matt Davis, Thomas Easterling, Jeanette Edelstein, Kristy Ellis, Moira Clarkin Evans, Charles Fischer, Marty Gephart, Kath Gibbs, Natalie Goldstein, Christina Gonzalez, Mamie Goodson, Nora Graham, Lindsay Griffith, Brenna Haffner, Joanna Hawkins, Elizabeth Haydel, Steve Hettleman, Cara Hoppe, Ashley Hymel, Carol Jago, Jennifer Johnson, Mason Judy, Gail Kearns, Shelly Knupp, Sarah Kushner, Shannon Last, Suzanne Lauchaire, Diana Leddy, David Liben, Farren Liben, Jennifer Marin, Susannah Maynard, Cathy McGath, Emily McKean, Jane Miller, Rebecca Moore, Cathy Newton, Turi Nilsson, Julie Norris, Galemarie Ola, Michelle Palmieri, Meredith Phillips, Shilpa Raman, Tonya Romayne, Emmet Rosenfeld, Jennifer Ruppel, Mike Russoniello, Deborah Samley, Casey Schultz, Renee Simpson, Rebecca Sklepovich, Amelia Swabb, Kim Taylor, Vicki Taylor, Melissa Thomson, Lindsay Tomlinson, Melissa Vail, Keenan Walsh, Julia Wasson, Lynn Welch, Yvonne Guerrero Welch, Emily Whyte, Lynn Woods, and Rachel Zindler.

Early Adopters

The following early adopters provided invaluable insight and guidance for Wit & Wisdom:

- Bourbonnais School District 53 • Bourbonnais, IL
- Coney Island Prep Middle School • Brooklyn, NY
- Gate City Charter School for the Arts • Merrimack, NH
- Hebrew Academy for Special Children • Brooklyn, NY
- Paris Independent Schools • Paris, KY
- Saydel Community School District • Saydel, IA
- Strive Collegiate Academy • Nashville, TN
- Valiente College Preparatory Charter School • South Gate, CA
- Voyageur Academy • Detroit, MI

Design Direction provided by Alton Creative, Inc.

Project management support, production design, and copyediting services provided by **ScribeConcepts.com**

Copyediting services provided by Fine Lines Editing

Product management support provided by Sandhill Consulting